Now We Will Speak in Flowers

Micki Blenkush

BLUE LIGHT PRESS
1st WORLD
PUBLISHING

San Francisco | Fairfield | Delhi

Now We Will Speak in Flowers

Micki Blenkush

Copyright ©2020 by Micki Blenkush

First Edition.

ISBN: 978-1-4218-3654-6

Library of Congress Control Number: 2020936127

1ST WORLD LIBRARY
PO Box 2211
Fairfield, Iowa 52556
www.1stworldpublishing.com

BLUE LIGHT PRESS
www.bluelightpress.com
Email: bluelightpress@aol.com

Author Photo: Lily Blenkush

Cover painting by Tammy Nara (*Flowerview: One of Each*)

CMAB
Central MN Arts Board

Thanks in part to a career development grant awarded by the Central MN Arts Board, funded by the McKnight Foundation, to help offset book design and promotional costs.

To Dan, for all the times

Contents

Unknown Beasts

Body as Birdhouse

May my silences become
more accurate.

– Theodore Roethke

Now We Will Speak in Flowers

Painted Cave

All week I've been crawling
the dirt floor of memory
trying to read flinty shapes

like calligraphy
in flickered light.
Inside-out, I move

through where I lived
before I knew of maps.
All that I think I know

can be traced to pattern.
I was primitive then,
working pigment to skin.

No-one sketches
the beasts
they already know.

Milky Blood Evidence

May Day

I pick dandelions from the generous field
enough to fill a kindergarten basket.
Folded construction paper, stapled handle.

I stand at the base of my neighbor's steps.
Wait for her to hobble out to thank me.
She pushes open the door, leans on her cane

without seeing the gift gracing her knob.
What do you want? she calls down her steps.
What game are you playing? she wants to know.

Her script expects some kind of trick.
I don't know my lines, but recognize
standing alone in the spotlight

of my making. Spilled dandelions
slowly closing. Their milky blood evidence
stuck between my fingers.

The Tower

What are the odds that I should live
blocks from the orphanage
where my father was housed?
The church where he knelt in the pews
folding his small hands
lifts its tower above the trees.

When the steeple was removed,
I spent weeks feeling the cleave
across my own forehead.
Look at that timespan of dreams:
falling, crumbling,
bombs in auditoriums –

I awaited each toppled wall, then cowered
beneath the sky's open portal.
I told my daughter, *Take all you can
but not too much to carry*
and tried to lead us back
to where we should belong.

The steeple finally returned
brimmed in new penny copper
to right the open field.
My home's terrain
was inhabited by my father
long before it was built.

He was blonde as a boy. Bird-boned
and navigating the river slope.
Collapse could be anything.
Machine sudden or time's calm ruin.
A ring of grit and stone
to someday dent the ground.

Daughter's Spring Rite

You lead us
through freshmelt mud
down the banks of the river
on this walk we've taken every spring
before ticks and poison ivy.

Your list of imagined animals
in need of rescue
grows longer than ever
in your tenth year.
Every hollow is a home
to fox, badger, mouse, or ant.

This sand you call soil
wraps your wrists
each time you reach past roots
and stillbrown life
spliced in erosion's wash.

One by one you hand to me
invisible creatures
I've learned to carry gently
over the slip of last year's leaves.
I ask how many more
beneath the staggering weight
of orphaned bears.

To the beaver-gnawed totem and back,
you seek the narrow gate.
Trees to climb, brambles to elude,
and moss I'm asked to touch
until I can feel
each tiny forest for its own distinct life.

There's ice like salt and ice like diamonds
riding the hasty current.
A windshield-wide pane of glass
pauses in the sleeping shallow until
we find a branch just long enough for you
to loosen it away.

Convent of Lived Things

Thrift store spoons, bought by the handful
and the daily morning sort
to find the one *M*-monogram
with the flowered swirl that feels just right,
textured stainless against my thumb.

My daughter requires the one wooden handle
whenever she has soup. Keeps us waiting,
food growing cold,
as she frets through the drawer.

O this fragile utensil tide. Chipped plates.
Thirty year t-shirts cut into rags.
Watercolor flea-market mug
bought from the turquoise-clad woman
I wanted to be. It's branching cracks
will someday leak, but for now it remains
the only cup for my tea.

My daughter once treasured a towel
with a frog-faced flap.
She wore it on her head after every bath
until one day she simply stepped from the tub
and dried off a different way.

The only time in our 28 years together
my husband ever asked *How could you*
was when I donated to Goodwill the fleece throw
that had bundled our cat
on his last trip to the vet.

I hadn't remembered,
had simply counted too many blankets
and squandered its essence.
Little cemeteries that we are.

Inside the Broken Year

August of 1990, my Godchild's baptism.
The President on CNN
announces a brand new war.
September of 1990, *I'm in the Twilight Zone,*
I tell my family. *It's me*
who has blown up the world.
The touch of those who act like mine
too much like a Taser
to my numb flesh. The pills they give
like static to my untuned mind.
Watch others watch me
lie upon the flowered couch,
unable to change the channel.
Inside and outside confused,
missiles and smart bombs the news.
Only in class sometimes words
mean something; this answer goes here.
Books like scaffolding help hold me together
yet the confusion of clothing
keeps me from leaving my bed.
On the day my shoes don't match
my own feet sail miles away beneath my desk.
For almost a year the panic of eating,

of not eating. Walking into traffic,
incomprehensible streetlights, cars.
Somehow abiding until August,
when I move alone to an old rundown house:
a borrowed bed, card table, folding chairs,
one channel on a black and white TV.
Wide open space where nothing –
not the freezer, the oven, or the toilet would work.
Each day the echo of my own feet
on scratched wood floors.

How it's Done

At first I thought
she was one of the aides.
How she kept one hand
in the pocket of her robe
like she held some key.

She was the one who told me
how I'd been brought in, panicked
for having blown up the world
until the injections
tempered the tinder
igniting my sights.

This woman lifted the foiled seal
from our packets of syrup
and poured it over pancakes
we ate with plastic forks.

Whether medication or madness,
my vision was fractured.
Noses drifted and mouths
could not still their tongues.

When I told the psychiatrist
that everything was cubist,
and he thought I meant communist,
she waved her scarred wrist
and said it didn't matter.

For 72 hours the trap of locks
and tempered glass
betrayed my frantic axis.
I paced the perimeter
of our penned space
as she paged through magazines.

I saw her weeks later,
crossing the outpatient parking lot.
She wore the kind of glasses
that darkened in the light,
but I like to think she saw me
when she tilted her head my way.

Successful Algorithms of Good Gone Power

was the title of the book
handed to me this morning
as I arrived this side of a dream.
At breakfast I told my daughter
of schools burned in foreign lands.
She paused in her reading
to let me talk of freedom
that began to taste like syrup
made cheap in a factory
from sweatshop labor.
I said nothing of stoning
or lynching or severing in any form.
This world is too small for children
who listen. I'm quiet again
inside the carapace I've grown.

Tell the String of Chromosomes Like a Rosary

Saturday mass then supper
at the corner café.
Grandma hunched to one side
as if pulled by the weight
of her purse

and now my mother
leans the same
even when she carries nothing.
On the phone,
she talks of bunions.

Tells of toes crossing
one another like twisted,
low-down promises.
She recalls Grandma's hammer toes,
her shoes to fit orthotics.

My own incantation
requires stretching every night.
Willing my curling grubs
to straighten, to soften
beyond conclusion.

Three days ago I woke limping
and it has not gone away.
Unexplained burning
beneath the soft dip
of my three outer toes.

Again I remove my shoe and look.
Push about my sole.
Try to feel something
between my smallest bones.

A Poem for Mary

Before, when I said prayer
I meant a memorized forgery of words.
Long ago, alone at 3:00 a.m., I don't know
if I was reciting the Hail Mary
or hissing aloud my collapse
like a balloon squeezed of breath.
You appeared as static. Sky blue robe
to match my childhood dresser figurine,
flashing in and out like a roller rink strobe
without the pulsing beat.
When the nurse came in, I knew not to mention.
I heard your silence, the holy distance.
Decades later, on retreat at a convent,
I hiked from every direction
to visit your likeness in the woods.
You of concrete, your foot upon the snake.
I don't know if this is who you are
and I don't know where to ask.
On my wall, where I forget to look,
you are framed as watercolor, an abstract aura.
I'm trying not to startle with each new pain.
If I'm desperate enough,
you will come again. Outside a church,

you are ceramic white, glowing
beyond your paint.
A man rests on the bench, eyes closed
beneath the open breadth of your palms.
I sit, parked in my car,
coveting another's statue.

Second Grade Summer

Ours was a town so small we were free
to ride our bikes inside borders
mapped by our parents.
Not near the hill of gravel
with the half-built house, nor past the school
nor the pasture with cows still exotic that year
before I moved to my stepdad's farm.
Up and down the grid of blocks
where we all lived: Jen and Kelly
and Kelly's brother Brad. I flew
my purple bike with the lift of a sparrow
past the orchard where the apples were as sour
as the deaf woman who watched,
leaning against her front porch.
Her lack of words chased us
to the ballfield where we rested
between the dugout's splintered walls,
listened for the call of dogs
who lunged against their own bent fences.
The longing in their circular howls
called us back to spark their rage once more.
We dared each other down that street,
then over a block to the yard with uncombed boys

pushing their rusted trucks through the dirt.
We coasted on pedals over smooth fresh tar.
Our legs were pistons fueled by Pop Tarts and Tang.
We rode for hours in the hot spread of summer
but not past the glow of streetlights
except that one time,
after which my bike was hung, off-limits
in our garage for weeklong penance.
Then I waited in my own yard
for the click of kickstands,
a sweep of voices.

Endlight

Seated in gray swivel chairs sharing tea
with a friend beneath the industrial sterility
of corporate phosphorescence, she declares
that all consciousness is light
about which I agree but don't want to admit
because it means that when in dying,
as my grandma shed the opaque fasteners
and began to gleam, I held fast
to the steal locker of my father's pain.
He wondered how anyone could have
let his mother work as a foster grandparent
at a shelter serving abused children.
I wondered how she actually was
baking cookies for the residents.
I could only see her measuring,
watching the clock, waiting to smoke.
Sitting with her in that hour of afternoon
on the day she later died was like glimpsing
a hem of sheer fabric, trying to imagine
how it could have been worn.
I would like to have asked her to model,
if not to mend. It was not so much
a fire from within but as if something

had taken down the gauzy baffling
so that the light allowed a glimpse
before the shadows burned into my retinas
like negatives for the sun.

Today Let Us Repair the Real Grass of Memory

We had one dog when I was a child,
a terrier when I was three.
I asked my father yesterday

what was his name
and neither of us could recall.
The dog's being has been lifted,

silent as a heron,
from my dioramaed mind.
All day I've been thinking

how he'd saved me from a bank of snow,
having barked finally long enough
to send rescue.

I'm working to fix a soft echo of fur
passed beneath my hand
behind the darkened glass.

Driving

Town girl transplant, too late
to learn this new language
of motors and gears. I was told to sit
where I knew I did not belong.
Turning the rusted wheel of the old Farmall
as my stepdad rode standing behind
grunting with the effort of patience
leaning around me to push this knob,
pull that lever shouting, *Let up*
on the clutch! Give it more gas!

Each time he told me to drive
straight across the field and back,
I knew nothing was that simple.
I could hear but not understand
words like throttle and clutch.
Could not grasp the timing of engines
left open to the wind.

The time I was sent to hitch an empty wagon,
I turned the wheel so sharply that I spun
backward clockwise, then overcorrected
to spin backward counterclockwise.

Round and round each direction
until my stepdad's *Jesus H. Christ*
roared even over the chug of his Allis Chalmers
as he stormed across the field.
He climbed up onto the Massey Fergusen
waved me down to hold the wagon hitch steady
as he smoothly backed the tractor into place.

From then on I was assigned to unload hay
or walk the fields picking rocks.
My stepdad stayed on the seat of the tractor,
hailing distant stones
to be lifted from the earth.

Even today on visits to the farm
I watch from afar
as my brother grinds feed and hauls bales.
His modern blue Ford looms out of place
against the rusted tractors
of memory, their strange song of names
still coursing through my mind.

Deer Hit

My daughter's face, ghastly in the headlight's glare
looking back through the windshield

to where I sit, trapped in the passenger seat
by the wedged front panel, watching her

shake her head, poised to bound into the woods
in search of the injured, tufts of hide

crammed between our headlight and bumper.
I monitor her upset while holding

a phone to my ear, cramped in my inability
to supervise my husband working to tie up the fender

or my daughter pacing past the pool of light
toward the harvested, unsheltering corn.

The insurance rep says it's been deer hit calls
all evening long and gives us a number for our claim.

My daughter weeps for the leaving behind.
Thirty miles per hour, fragments rattling.

Cartography of Ruins

I slow my drive
past the abandoned gravel pit
where, as we were growing up
the trees and shrubs
had not yet taken over

and we could still climb
the lilt of land
carved by machines
into bowls and hills unlike anything
formed in nature.

Then we measured the earth
in newborn snakes,
against the weight
of buttercups carried home
in drooping bouquets.

Now from the road,
the canopy of trees grown taller
than when we squeezed
between them
at the entrance of long ago.

Gone must be
the hollows where we sat
on our first picnic of spring,
dainty as teacups
on the still-brown grass

peeling Easter eggs
across the damp soil,
leaving shells scattered
in pastel mosaic offering
to gods we wanted to know.

Utensil Tide

Awake that Requires the Night

There's a nocturnal bent
I'm trying not to court.
Whispers of words repeated
after the first crash of sleep.
Midnight, 1:30, 2:15 and on
until finally I rise to scribe.

My grandmother was bipolar
in the days they called it crazy.
Shock treatments in a locked ward
long before I met her.

I recognized the way
her face received instruction
in order to smile.
Her monotone voice
spoke through my throat.

The only time she referenced
her moon-tone madness was when
my father brought her to visit
my own mental health unit
when I was twenty-two.

She said a doctor had told her
never to stop crafting.
Indeed she gifted needlepoint
to anyone she knew
well into her 90s.

I trade away sleep for rockets
and daisies stitched with the genius
of 3:00 a.m. Toppled later
to pipe cleaners, limp with wet paste.
In the milky wash of dawn,
fallen down.

What the Neighborhood Says

A house left peeling
in sloughed-off patches
a public wish
for a mask of siding.

Burnished death of green
the name for ferns
left to freeze
in summer pots.

A seedling poking through
the rotted garage wall
announces I will grow
no matter how you leave.

Trinkets like gumdrops
scatter a yard --
A fractured capsule,
overdone.

Facing a chair
to a fence of stone
is a careless act --
a gaping thing
not put back.

Constellations

The week before they close the Lake George rink
we gaze into Milky Way bubbles
trapped beneath layers of ice
as you would any galaxy about to die.

Stirred with a fire needing to burn,
I widen arcs around my family.
My daughter kneels as if to court the fish
trapped below. Shining schools

she would name and train
and rescue from all peril.
Her gravity moves her father
in narrow ellipses

around the warmth of their laughter
as he shows her how to skate backward.
She faces the wind,
curves her feet like an hourglass.

She turns in sharp angles
before falling with snowpants-padded whumps.
I squeeze the hood around my neck
to protect from bite of wind,

skate faster to keep warm.
My husband and I touch mittens
in silent passing.
I focus on small cracks

for they will trip you every time.
Beyond the scratched surface of the ice,
I see dendrites and neurons.
Microscoped slides of a mind viewed close

rather than the webbed dimensions
of the universe. The one time I fall,
I'm careful to go down slow.
As the wind spins me into sideways spiral,

one gloved hand reaches in a dangle
that feels almost graceful,
like a shooting star
before its soft descent.

Changing Schools

I stood before blank faces
as the teacher spoke my name.
I squeaked the lid of an empty desk,
rattled pencils into place.

When it came my turn to read,
words tangled on the map of my tongue.
In gym I learned that planning to catch kickballs
from a field of fresh new friends
was like expecting to drill for water
before finding a land too parched,
runners too fast to tag.

I might have been a dowser,
though the word was buried deep
in dictionaries squeezed
along the bottom shelves,
leaving space above
for girls to move their Barbies
through imagined houses
after we drank our morning milk.

One girl dangled a spare Barbie before my eyes
and said I could borrow it for the day.
Then she turned to tell the others
where theirs should live among the shelves.

I held that doll before me
as I inched across the linoleum,
divining my position.

This is the Route

that I lumbered through my daughter's infancy.
Pushing her stroller in search
of a better sidewalk, needing
a rhythmic drone to soothe us both.

Ten years later, I leave her
with a job to clear the table
from clutter she's piled for months
as I walk to calm myself alone.

This is the summer she wants to roam
with the neighbor girl
who arrives daily on our deck
to show her afar.

Here's the cul-de-sac we used to take.
Clockwise, then counter-clockwise
to catch the ultimate sectioned sidewalk
that never failed to lull her asleep.

Every mother is the expert of her own
until she's not. The morning glory fence
has been bare for years, but it's still that
inside my mind.

Almost home through the patch of woods
that took hours to cross
when she first climbed from her stroller
to show me every leaf.

As I near, I catch the creak
of our front door even though I told her
not to leave
or let anybody in.

When I ask what she was doing,
she stands at her almost-clear table
to say she'd found some natural things
to toss loose across the field.

Déjà Vu

I mentioned to my Mom
the time she'd yelled to me
through the glass
of the locked garage door.
I was alone in the house
and three years old.

I remember the confusion --
she holding the long board
hands waving me back
the shattering, she walking in
over broken glass
me not afraid, now safe.

When she said,
That never happened
I didn't tell her,
the look on her face
was the same
as when she tried to talk
through the glass
of the locked door.

Cutting Board

Heavier than it needs to be. Inch and a half thick
and long as my arm. A blunted arrow
with a carved hole that wants to be an eye.

A thing good enough. No fast mechanics.
Routines of salad. Of potatoes
by their means.

Oak or maple. Hewn in a forgotten land
then donated in time for us to set up house.
How little we had. Propped on a kitchen counter.

A galaxy of marks made in distracted thoughts
of what comes next or someone running late.
Deeper scars take weeks or months.

A surface fine to mar. Swept away
in faint shreds. Only the edge
retains a honeyed shine.

A thing named for what it does.
The familiar two-step heft
of picking it up and setting it down.

To the High School Friend Who Messages Me on Facebook Then Takes So Long to Respond

This is how I've kept myself here
since you last saw me two decades ago
at our ten-year reunion. That night
when I smoked again so long past quitting,
woke the next day on my parent's couch,
returned to my husband who steered
my hungover canoe around the pond
all afternoon. At first I can think of nothing
more to say. For almost a week
I wonder what you'd see
in my garden's daily weeds. I want to tell you
how the first surprise of line-dried towels
plays rough against my skin as I step
outside the fresh steam of my shower.
I still imagine your seventeen-year-old self
walking alongside me. Doing things
we'd not have imagined as we rode
the gravel roads, watched for cops,
tossed empty cans into ditches.
I want to speak for you some word
like trowel as I lift one from the tangle
of my garage. Show the way
I kneel and dig.

The What of It

Those little tractor yard sprinklers —
how do they work?
Whenever I catch a glimpse
I'm soothed like a hammock
held by an amicable thing.

I don't think about this enough:
vital elements willing to move
in primary order
miniature vehicles built to appear
inevitable.

This one painted yellow
casting low arcs of water
preventing death
of grass, reminding that tomorrow
is the spit-shine of today.

Not an object to carry but to follow,
tethered to a hose.
Nothing but small adjustments
to a set perimeter
learned by trial and error.

A Cargo of Perspective

Everything they had was borrowed; they had nothing of their own at all.
— Mary Norton, <u>The Borrowers</u>

I'm thinking about the state of the world
like it's a place to someday visit.
When I was a child,
I wanted most to shrink.
To meet Arrietty behind the walls,
learn how she made do.
Thread and postage stamps.
Paucity here. Usefulness there.
There are forces taking sides
and we're missing the little things.
When you're small, a thimble
can hold enough.
Playing card empire.
A needle for a spear.

A Woman's Weight

In this mid-life metabolism
every half-donut near the copier at work
matters in a whole new way.
Pants purchased two years ago
threaten now to no longer fit.
Though when I shake them out
and bend and squat, trying
to stretch back in, I can still evoke
the knife-edge lure of hip-bones
verified for months upon waking.
This is one kind of insulation.
The other arrives in creeps and hefts.
Sour cream pancakes, caramel French toast,
every common indulgence.
My mouth becomes a suckerfish
cleaning along the bottom edge
until I grow once more thick as a mattress
and tiresome with inventory
of all that has and may be eaten.
It took forty pounds heavier than this,
back at the age of twenty,
before I could perceive numbers on a scale
and admit to something other

than the shrinking conspiracy of my clothes.
If I push against failure hard enough,
I can form my cells into wanting nothing
but the can't and the won't.
At the age of twenty-two,
twenty pounds lighter than now,
I passed mirrors dismayed to still detect
the outline of my legs
floating the bag of my jeans.
Who might I be
without the pulling in
and pushing away?
The pendulum is slowing.
It has taken decades to rest
inside my skin. Some mornings
I lie still and awake
before billowing my hopes
upon the sail.

Unanswered

In the dream, a guy who'd died
driving himself into a guardrail
thirty-two years ago sits next to me.
But do you feel? he asks
and each time I try to move
further down the bench,
he lifts a blanket over us both
as though to protect from rain.
He's sober now, strange without
the Jack Daniels tipping back
to the gravity of empty.
Only you can say, he says,
shifting the blanket around.
What I've always wanted to know,
but still don't ask,
is whether he'd meant to die.
I know silence, he says,
then nothing more
as we huddle together
at the far end of the bench.

The Golden Hour

Three years ago, with the help of WebMD
I diagnosed the pain in my side as liver cancer,
the confusion in my brain a tumor.
Not having long to live lifted the winter gray weight
almost like when I was seven
in each last hour of summer twilight
crawling beneath the lilacs
knowing that when the streetlights came on
we'd all have to go home.

Back then, when my babysitter promised
a scavenger hunt
then read through the windshield of his glasses
as though driving the western plains,
I knew I had to do something.
Had to scamper at his feet
folding clues into torn squares
so he would not forget I was there.

Three years ago, when I was sent from doctor
to specialist and returned
from the tunnels of MRIs unscathed,
it felt like that same summer
when my mother stood in the yard
arranging garage sale vases and votives --
spraying each item into gold,
sparkling the grass all around.

Secondhand Holy Man

I need a shaman wearing borrowed clothes.
Someone versed in tarnish and rust
who knows

all things settle as they are
including what enters the side door
in boxes and bags.

There must be some incantation
for delivering discards from my home:
picture frames splintered

but not quite broken,
shoes that never fit, unmatched Tupperware
unable to seal anything.

He'll appear among the racks
hanging worn-out shirts and pants
as I search for dishes to make a set.

Anonymous, he'll walk the aisles
sifting clutter, shining fragments
suitable to keep.

Heft

A pit near the farm where I grew up
holds stones culled from fields
every spring before planting.

Granite, shale, and slate
lifted from the earth
then dumped out of sight

or carted off in pockets
by we who believed
picking rocks is part selection.

The stone that anchors my desk
holds a formula of minerals
I do not know, but its weight

speaks to my blood. Her shape
suggests a fish. Scarified marks
of saxophone ears and fallen chin.

She is toothless old. No sound
but not silence either. A red note
that rises in my hand.

Unknown Beasts

Impervious

Locks on all the doors
and a windowed enclosure
from which nurses buzzed in visitors
who emerged like apparitions
from behind the mesh.

My family arrived to find me
seated with new kin:
patients in matching robes,
our feet in grippy slippers
propped upon a row of chairs.

Even though my father warned
not to make these my people,
I bummed cigarettes from a guy
with ravens in his eyes.
I exchanged numbers with a woman
trailing confetti from her sleeves.

When I asked for my make-up,
my stepmom brought the whole bin.
Wrong-shadowed shades
I'd neglected to throw away
painted on in layers.

In-Home Assessment

What are your primary health concerns?

Fleeting momentum of bicycles.
TVs in the windows of my neighbors.
A sandwich of scene
outside my reach.

How well do you sleep?

Best intentions braided and left to fray
like woven birds of thread.
Peacock feather broken in the street.
Knees bent in a crouch
before the approaching car.

Do you see or hear things that others don't?

To be a pilgrim or put on a costume.
When it rains, clothes left on the line
grow wet from the bottom up.

Is there someone we may call in case of emergency?

The grocery clerk who wears a rosary
asked if I found what I needed.

Are you able to care for yourself and home?

Red, the color of passing.
Tire ruts through clover.
Blanket of welcome. Fear of crying
in your presence.

If you could no longer live here, where would you like to live?

Rain clinging to pine needles
in a just-washed evening. Turrets and towers.
Clipboards and protractors. What the tools
need the people to do.

As Above, So Below

On the shore of Lake Superior,
my daughter and I explore
the beach. She rescues
a minnow from where it flopped
partially submerged in shallow canal.
Suggests we make for him a museum,
so he can enjoy his new home
within the shoreline rock.
We gather the most interesting sticks
to stagger around the edge, save the best
birch bark to float upon his surface.
She gently lowers agates
right into the water
so he can get a close-up look
at sparkles, worn smooth.
As the fog burns to steam
we drain our canteen. Look again
along the shore for stones
in select colors, shapes.
Though we've lost our minnow
somewhere beneath the specter
of floating bark, we continue
adding to the museum's border.

Now an intricate earthy brocade,
a loose yet evident boundary
inviting future visitors to come closer.
See this special something,
marked so, here in the open.

Bottomland Notebook

Backyard of garter snakes stretched down to soggy marsh.
My father left slices of death behind the mower.

Up a hill alone to kindergarten. Red-marked worksheets
strewn free from my bag.

Sideburns and shag carpet. Gray fuel of smoke.
My mother at the sink. At the stove.

My father's beercan collection shelved library neat.
A rusted nail passed through my shoe.

Mutual of Omaha's Wild Kingdom. Predator. Prey.
Bitten by a mouse that I wrestled from our cat.

My mother in blue robe, crying over another pending move.
I threw toys down the stairs to blame my baby sister.

My uncle ran alongside my first bike, sailed me loose
across the snake-dead grass.

Variables

The man who stands at the corner
holding the *Homeless, Please Help* sign
is different. Even if he is the same guy,
today he is lifting one foot to the other
though it really isn't that cold.
The traffic moves, so you forget
until later at your desk when you hear
a bang so thunderous it shakes your house.
You open blinds to look out all four sides
but no one is crashing into anything anywhere.
You don't see anyone at all, so you think
of that episode of *The Twilight Zone*
where the man is the only soul left on earth,
and it isn't until the next day when you see
the lumber dumped in your neighbor's yard
that you figure it was the unloading.
What they'll be building remains to be seen,
because you don't want to stand in the street
counting beams and trusses, and there is nothing
you can do anyway. The homeless guy and the lumber
and the journals you've been meaning to burn
are each still out there. The night you dream
of walking on a roof high above your current city,

you wake holding the word *communion*
in your mouth. Its flavor lingers as you slice the fruit.
You pack lunches as it dissolves, pressed
like a wafer against your tongue.

Continuing the Mystery of Unfound Things

In second grade I steered my best friend
around the playground
as though we were both on safari.
We shuffled in spring boots
while I pointed to trash emerging
from beneath the melting snow
as promised revelation.

There were no ordinary gum wrappers.
No arbitrary newspapers
wedged beneath hapless shrubs.
Each day I commented on the lean
of fence posts, a half-buried glove,
sticks piled beneath the slide.

For two weeks just she and me alone
walking the edge of the playground
until a smashed can led us
to the monkey bars
where we climbed until the next thing
steered us somewhere new.

When Joann grew bored
I hid a piece of bark
in the teacher's Kleenex box,
then feigned surprise
at the back of the room during math.
I crayoned *Keep Looking* in blocky letters,
left it under her coat.

After she joined her other friends
on the ordinary swings,
I penciled letters on a block of wood
professing love, of all things,
for Ricky the neighbor boy
then buried it in the sand.

I denied my own script
when his sister dug it up
and held it high
above her head.

New Year's Morning

Alone at the kitchen table
with my breakfast and resolutions,
a tap against glass
announces a nuthatch
perched on the outer sill.
Only he and distant city lights
against a foreground of dark
on a twenty-below-zero morning.
The bird tilts his head, cranes his neck
as if trying to peer inside.
Not quite focusing on me sitting right here
before he flies away to some distant tree
or nest of leaves. Soon another tap
lifts my eyes from cereal
to find him trying
to fly right through the window
despite the Christmas decals
making all the more obvious
the solid barrier between.
He keeps disappearing into the dark,
then reappearing
as a smash against glass.
Not hard enough to injure

but forceful, like wanting an answer
before I can understand the question.
I notice too my own reflection,
stern as my grandpa whenever he waited
another's turn playing cards.
What is to be done?
I hear no words in the syllables of beak
as the bird pecks
all four corners of the window
in a final attempt to gain entry.

2-West

I who thought the night-nurse was my aunt Mary
and who by turns believed I was pregnant,
dying as a martyr, and had launched nuclear missiles

across the arc of the earth, held items
brought by my visitors as though
they'd raft me up

over first the flood of delusion
then the drown of medication
that walked me like a puppet.

My boyfriend brought a mix-tape
which I tried to discern through headphones
beneath the fluorescence of my psych-ward room.

My mother delivered handmade cards
from my sister and brother. *Get well, We miss you*
crayoned between balloon and sun.

My stepmom brought an afghan.
A blanket to rest me still
rather than pace the walled edges.

My father delivered his assertion,
This is not One Flew Over the Cuckoo's Nest
when I fomented agitation.

On the night my visitors coaxed me through
a game of dominoes, I chewed an entire pack
of cough drops from my stepmom's purse.

After months of my wasting away,
the reptilian bean of my brain sought survival
in a register of real while eating.

The next-day message left for my now-husband
remains a catch-phrase still:
Bring me all the Lifesavers you can afford.

Some of What I Found and Lost, Ages 15 to 20

A boy in a red bandana
who said *Thistledew* so pretty
it made me want to visit
next time he went to juvie.
The periodic table. List of prepositions.
Generic cigarettes slipped
from the bottom of my mother's carton.
Horror films. Driving any tractor.
Liquors in Easter hues
hidden among the cleansers
beneath the kitchen sink.
Skinny cats in ballpoint ink
tattooed across the backs of my hands.
Rolling out the passenger side
of my friend's car into the littered ditch
as she was still driving. Cuts on my face
to understand upon waking.
My first college roommate
who went to bed by ten.
Microwaved Bisquick stirred with sugar.
Popcorn eaten by the dry handful for dinner.
The pulse of party-house floors.
Classes half awake.

Biology test with weeds in my hair
after riding through the quarries
on the back of some guy's motorbike.
A lofted bed in an upstairs room
during summer of record heat.
Protest buttons armoring my jacket.
Some dearth of myself,
the fabric between.

Sunday Morning

In the crowded lobby of the pancake house,
we hold our pagers like crucibles.
The woman next to me hums a looping tune,
plays her electronic Scrabble.
She asks if she's crowding me on the bench,
not if I mind the hum.
I look around, each of us dripping
from the pour of Sunday rain,
trust that soon we'll all be beckoned forth.
The hostess says it plain each time
the door opens, at least a sixty-minute wait.
Quiet facts added to the sediment
of life's terrain: the squish inside our shoes,
another lost umbrella,
somewhere else a mother frying bacon.
The hum of the woman who won't stop
a raft to sail the coming hour.

For the Students of Senior Picture Season

Stone Arch Bridge, Minneapolis

Each of you staged by turns
before the mill's artful ruins
and the upswept spray
of the dam-spilled river.

Someone carries a change of clothes,
a comb, your metaphorical placement.
You in newly-distressed jeans,
the store's folded crease

crisp against the offhand pose.
Your indelible image high above
the graffiti-graced relics
and shadowed trails.

Your tense jaw poised to smile
when the shutter finally opens.
Archways, railings, lavish jam of logs
across the crouched falls.

You hunched on the curb,
outside the frame,
one hand atop your sprayed 'do
while the photographer stages

a light reflector
against the cloud-drowned sun.
Not the wind but your wind
shedding loose October trees.

Council for Revival

cacophony of voice: feathered and furred

What you might call ratcheting.
Weave the way that we do,
twigs and bits of yarn. Body
as a birdhouse. Scavenge.
Born into a shape. Die from a shape.
Carcass is never the same.
Track your prints
to and from the woods.
Watch my flutter or don't.
The pin drop of my heart.
The dirt, the burrow.
Your necessary home.
Bristled layers. Tug from the roots.
Kick and chew.
Claw your way down.

We Have Need for This

The first thing
I remembered to see
after the forsaken prayer
to look through the eyes of God
was the German Shepherd
prancing up on ballerina legs
fighting against his leash.

Each hair bristled to sunlit attention
as he lunged left then right.
Ears steepled to holy invitation,
torpedo nose sniffing
past the human limits
of today's exquisite breeze.

The woman who never looked down
as she shifted the leash
hand to hand
against the justifiable strain.

Riding the Hurricane at the Minnesota State Fair

My daughter chooses one last ride
to finish our twelve-hour day.
We agree on tight spins inside lilting loops
with a chance to press our heads back
against the rests.

Just before it all begins, we're joined
by two young men in backward caps,
tattoos up their freckled arms.
Both with Down's Syndrome,
they move like brothers as they buckle in
for the ride.

As soon as the music starts,
the one just to my right leans forward
raises both arms in perfect sync
to the rap beat. He sings all the words,
has seen all the videos. He knows how to move,
how to nod to the crowd. He never leans back,
so we languish in simple turns.

To my left, my daughter's sleepy eyes
reflect the dawning midway lights.
She doesn't seem to care
we're not spinning in the fast way,
so I quell the urge to ask
that the man lean back.

I watch him work his distant stage
and next to him, the quiet friend
who tilts his head forward
to gaze upon his own cupped hand
lifted just above his eyes
as if to hold still our center.

Passing Through the Thicket

I should know by now
not to use the locker in the corner
where I have to sidle between
half-naked water aerobics ladies at the gym
dressing as an afterthought
to talk of children, cancer treatments,
and dementia-addled spouses.
One lays a towel on which to sit.
The crack of her butt a Friday morning fact
as her friend spreads lotion
across her back and shoulders
and together they re-chorus
the stop-start conversation
as each woman returns from the mirror
or fresh and dripping
from her long-winded shower.
Some walk around in nothing but a bra
while others start with the bottom half
letting their breasts sway and dangle
as they bend to tie their shoes.
How many lives have they led?
Bellies in a range of pallor and scar.

Wolves

At dinner I told my daughter
about a story heard on the radio
of a woman chased up a tree by wolves
as her dog was left on the ground.
How the woman screamed for her pet to run

but the dog only whimpered
and pawed at the trunk
as the wolves circled near.
Then the woman remembered
to call through her tears

all her thankful love
as the dog continued to reach and whine.
Soon the woman noticed
that the wolves had stopped to sit,
vigilant in a circle.

Without a sound or glance,
the wolves all stood, took five steps back,
then sat again. They repeated as they retreated,
finally allowing the woman to descend
and clutch her unharmed pet.

Silently, my daughter put down her fork
then got up from the table
to sit on her haunches.
She cocked her head as if to listen
for mercy's silent scratch.

Body as Birdhouse

Rehearsal for Becoming Swallowed

Motility of dry fountain leaves,
hosta's green-rooted cling,
and ornamental grass knocked flat
by mid-November snow.
If everything is fallow, anything is fallow.
All that bloom before the shrivel.
Unable to remember the correct
spill of vines from pillared urns
or where hollyhock nostalgia
had been cornered.
If I hadn't already known
the white garden, I'd have no reason
to figure-eight the sections
searching for something other
than silver frost to littered foliage,
the low sun playing shadows
against the clipped rectangle hedge,
and barren soil left to freeze
in rough, uneven pause.

Map Not to Scale

When she leaves, she takes:
bike helmet, watch,
and sometimes
a tied-shut backpack.

I could not tell you her routes
only that she returns
to hear me run my words
up and down
every surface of our home.

Don't push back on that door.
Don't bang and jump
or smear your hands
along the hall.

The smart snap
of Rubbermaid container
in the palm of her hand.
Vases she makes from jars
to hold the feathers she gathers
from capacious fields.

I watch her stand in the leaking
cold light of the fridge
without telling her to close the door
the way you'd wait for a deer
to cross a meadow.

Two Ships, Long Marriage

What, if anything, can be said when you arrive
at 4:00 a.m. to our bed where I have stalked alone
into dreams I would have preferred to share
but instead you've lingered
in the unheated basement,
drafting from your lucid mind
plans for a workshop
you began to sketch in the corner of our den
during a movie selected by our daughter
(which, by our simple glance five minutes in,
we both could have lived without)
and I, who'd long lain awake in menopausal steam
thinking poems I'd like to write,
now silently welcome you
to whatever warmth
I'll leave behind.

Clean

Let it go long enough
and you learn to see past
some of the mess. All those years
dusting door frames, wiping webs
from backs of bookshelves
amounted to nothing
but fleeting virtue. Anyone can work
with rags and water. What about
some real transformation? Forgive yourself
often enough and you start to forget
the way clean once felt.
All the way all at once clean
with counters gleaming,
when even a small stack of papers
suggested untended corners
so was quickly shuffled away.
Once my closets held only the things
I needed. Now dried beans age
in my cupboard, wait
for the promise of soup.
Through unwashed windows
I watch June's tide of maple seeds
spin to the ground, hands empty
at my side.

A Body in the Body of the Universe

When I went hungry, I slept less.
Roused by hummingbirds at 4:00 a.m.
to add sugar to my blood.
Today, I rest to the luxury of dozing,
wait for news of our survival. Slow bleed
of light around the shades,
my mind's graffitied chug like box cars on a train.
That my skin cracks open feels significant.
Forced air heat blasting through the vents.
I buy jugs of distilled water
to feed my humidifier, take too-long showers
mouth agape, inhaling the steam.
Persistent itch, abrasion with bullhorn,
subcutaneous alarm.

Elegy with Misplaced Props

Sunday Drive, my father at the wheel
back to 1975 Grey Eagle, Minnesota
to find the rambler my parents built
just before they divorced.
Past overgrown trees superimposed
on bareness that was, Masonite siding
now painted blue, garage bashed in.
Then, me posed on the front steps
in first communion dress. Year of
my mother's cucumber pore-cleansing mask.
My father's sawdust and varnish.
My sister and I taking turns hiding bracelets
across the new-development grass.
Look, I say, showing my daughter
the silvered scar on the arch of my foot.
Glass embedded while wading the holding pond,
here where this parking lot is.
Town five blocks wide, free to roam
graveled edge to graveled edge
laced with white-flowered weeds
I tasted and claimed to be sugar.
After we moved to my stepdad's farm,
we returned one weekend per month.

Salt metallic of my stepmother's canned peas.
Sliced diagonal of her buttered toast.
She and my dad papered my room in pink and blue
for the baby that never came
before they moved to Arizona.
In 1987, passing through, I found Kelly,
daughter of McDermond's Grocery, working the till.
Whether she remembered me
was all I asked, and now the store is gone.
Today my dad drives around looking
beyond houses to where a park should be
for the stagecoach on which he'd posed us for pictures.
I crane my neck until I spot the coach
past the shrunk-down tennis courts.
My dad says it's rusted and in the wrong place.
I maintain they've moved its rickety frame.
My stepmom suggests that someone
simply get out for a closer look.
It isn't the same, my dad concludes
backing up the car.

Faltered

I can see by the fresh startle
in my grandmother's eyes that she's slipping
from this earth. All my words float up

and pop like bubbles
before she can grasp
the luster of their meaning.

When I mention the needlepoint crafts
she used to make, my grandma looks confused,
shakes her head like she can't imagine.

My voice rises against her mumble.
All those gifts of coasters and placemats
were her beauty, her faltered focus

away from the ten children
she raised and estranged with bruises
and battles carried into her 93rd year.

I'm the oldest daughter of her oldest son.
She wants me to tell her where he is,
what he's doing. Her voice an accusation

I cannot answer, still trying to manage the high-wire act
of sitting in this room on a folding chair.
When my daughter shows the frayed yarn cat

on the table near her bed,
and grandma says, *I never did that*,
my silence settles like a shroud.

Lake George Flux

It takes showing up
to see the fugue
between freeze and thaw.
Last month ice skating
and today an open furrow of melt
allows the ducks to swim a moat
beyond where citizens have tossed
sticks and rocks,
trying to break through.

The ducks stand on the edge
and preen beneath their wings
while behind them on the ice
twigs and stones cast impressions
burned by the sun.

Every year the thaw reveals
new patterns --
alien spiders or fireworks
emerge then fade
like underdeveloped film.

Overcast slush
folds into streaks of light
as though stirred by a giant ladle,
while transitory circles
confess a hidden vortex
beneath November's first freeze.

It takes a couple walks
around the lake to notice
a parable of footprints.
Each impression bubbles up
as though past-pressured steps
could release them back to float
across the unlocked water.

When I Was Young and Yet More Hollow

I chewed raw macaroni, uncooked oats,
dry field corn from a cob.
I gnawed sleeves, collars,
and nibbled away erasers.
I pulled threads from sweaters,
spun them against my mouth's roof
like dialing a compass, then pressed
the acute tang of Play-Dough,
its misshapen, any-colored fruit
deep into my cheek.
Someone later said I wouldn't have
licked a frozen metal bridge
that spanned the creek
on my route to kindergarten
unless another suggested.
There is a version where I wasn't alone.
Where I didn't, fearing late,
summon strength to rip away the hidden
texture of my hunger. Rust and blood
a badge upon my tongue.

Elegy for the Men of My Stepfather's Town

Every time my stepfather asks
if I remember Gordy or Lloyd or some other
lifelong, smalltown acquaintance --
Dead, he'll say, rolling his neck

as he taps out a cigarette.
What do they die of? Heart mostly.
Congestion or lack. Weathered years
in seedcaps and pickup trucks.

Larry who sold hardware
went tethered to oxygen
after the store burned
to the ground.

Calvin spent weeks measuring paneling
to hang in my parents' stairwell
only to shoot himself in the head
after he finished the job.

Leroy the veterinarian,
who drank coffee at our table
after tending a cow's mastitis
sailed away on dementia's slow raft.

Some names I only pretend to recognize.
Context of coffee shops so crowded
we kids had to lean against the wall,
picking sugar from our napkins.

Others must have slipped
without my notice.
Mr. Munson, playground supervisor.
Ferdie who delivered gas.

Men who loomed old
forty years ago.
Men like dowels.
Like mortar to brick.

Love Letter to the Crowd

You try to stay anonymous
but today there's a child screaming
as he's bustled through the butterfly house
red-faced and kicking shoeless
while his father tries to block the hands
that punch against the flutters
and the rest of us look to one another's eyes
to raise some kind of verdict
as we do when the large woman
who dances at the concert's edge
becomes a parachute of color,
gyrating and somersaulting
through the blur of us.
Let's make a record of this:
zoos, fairs, and parades when no one rises
with a gun or drives a van
into our nameless mass.
Today a mother walks to the parking lot
waggling her fingers --
a lure for the child who toddles behind,
arms outstretched, laughing
through your crowded heart.

Witness

Beyond my neighbor's fence,
not a field of tulips, but enough.
A quorum of red and yellow
all along my vision's canvas.

At night I hear them best.
Buds folded in a murmur,
metronome without the tick
nodding in softlit breeze.

The geomancy of sovereign, yin
as the waning moon --
a fleeting congregation
unconcerned with rule.

Just before their petals stumble loose
around each barren stem, they open
to their fire-eater fullest --
tilting back, looking up.

Fort of Ice and Snow

Warm days after so much snow
invited industry.
My daughter left boulders
high as her fourth-grade shoulders
strewn about the field
like a midwest Stonehenge
until on the weekend
her father helped to move them
all together.

Her dream of a simple tunnel
widened to a room-size fort
complete with salvaged wood
for shelves and a sturdy roof
to protect from birds of prey
when they pretended as mice
to shape morsels for their larder.
I could barely see their outlines
when I called them in from foggy dusk.

At first light we saw the trampled pile.
Footprints around crushed ruin.
Shelves stabbed into snow
like relics from a razed temple
in a torn land.

To have no balm for her mourning.
No answers to who and why.
Only the what of collapse
by someone who'd watched
before night arrived
to blanket the field.

What prayer might we offer
such willful destruction?
I speak of sun and melt
as she plans
to build again.

Now We Will Speak in Flowers

I.

As a child I let the train of my own focus
roar across the tracks of my mother's words
when she returned from the garden
elbow deep in dirt sprouting:

clematis   *four o clocks*   *hosta.*

Squirrels digging tulips, dogs trampling
marigolds, even her confession
to pulling daisies like common weeds
a mumbled blur. Not until the day she showed me
bright candy flowers I could cut into my own bouquet
did I accept one name. Zinnia, my mind whispered
as I bent low snipping off extra leaves, stroking
the layered petals like feathers down
a pigeon's breast.

II.

Following her stroke, we brought flowers
to my mother's room. Sweeping gestures
said all her smiling mouth could not. The first texts
she ever sent to me came from the hospital.
Simple *love you's* floating back and forth
across January nights. Soon she texted flowers
across the distance. Gerber daisies
in a pixilated square.

Hopeful talk of morning glories germinated
as her speech gradually returned.
I walked the floor of my own house,
gripping the phone, straining to understand.
When I asked how deeply to plant
the four o' clock seeds she gave me last fall,
their name sprang like a reflex
from my mouth.

III.

In late July she makes her first drive alone to visit.
We join the other tourists walking the paths
of Munsinger Gardens:

    Dianthus I say, gesturing near her feet.

Coleus, she says, nodding just ahead.

    Calla lily? I ask.

Canna lily, she says.

Stopping at all benches so she can catch her breath
we look past the fountains, past others
also pointing, naming.

    Alium, we murmur

as my daughter flits from flower to fountain
    and back again to us.

Nearby the verbena nods. Salvia sways.

Delphinium, we croon
    to anyone who might listen

    lobelia   *hydrangea*   *fern*

Notes

"Tell the String of Chromosomes" owes its title to a line by Kathryn Kysar

"A Poem for Mary" is after "A Poem for God" by Geffrey Davis

"Convent of Lived Things" owes its title and final line to Rilke, as translated by Anita Barrows and Joanna Macy

"In-Home Assessment" owes its structure to sam sax's "Description for Police"

"Bottomland Notebook" is after Keith Ekiss

Acknowledgements

Thank you to editors and staff of the following journals in which the following poems first appeared, some in slightly different form:

Adanna: "A Woman's Weight," and "Map Not to Scale"

CAGIBI: "New Year's Morning"

Clementine Unbound: "Painted Cave"

Crab Creek Review: "Elegy with Misplaced Props"

Gravel: "Continuing the Mystery of Unfound Things"

Gyroscope Review: "A Cargo of Perspective," "Constellations," "Now We Will Speak in Flowers," "To the High School Friend...," "Unanswered," and "Variables,"

Heron Tree: "*As Above, So Below*," *and* "Cartography of Ruins"

Metafore: "Lake George Flux," and "Witness"

Midway Journal: "Bottomland Notebook," "Endlight," "Faltered," and "When I was Young and Yet More Hollow"

Muddy River Poetry Review: "Changing Schools"

Naugatuck River Review: "Driving"

Nebo: "Convent of Lived Things"

One Sentence Poems: "Two Ships, Long Marriage"

Pittsburgh Poetry Review: "In-Home Assessment"

Postcard Poems and Prose Magazine: "May Day"

Red Coyote: "Awake that Requires the Night," and "Some of What I Found and Lost
Ages 15 to 20"

Sequestrum "Clean"

Star 82 Review: "Sunday Morning"

South 85 Journal: "Tell the String of Chromosomes Like a Rosary"

The Talking Stick -- Jackpine Writers' Bloc anthology: "Fort of Ice and Snow"

Typishly: "Elegy for the Men of My Stepfather's Town"

West Texas Review: "Daughter's Spring Rite"

Zingaria Poetry Review: "A Body in the Body of the Universe"

Thank you to Blue Light Press for selecting this work for publication.

Thank you to the Loft Literary Center and the Jerome Foundation for the 2017 – 2018 Mentor Series Fellowship. The

camaraderie and wisdom of all the mentors and fellow partic-
ipants were priceless. Thanks especially to local mentor Jen-
nifer Kwon Dobbs and fellow poets Hallie Wiederholdt, Preeti
Kaur, and Jasmin Ziegler whose input helped shape this man-
uscript.

Thank you to the Central MN Arts Board and the McKnight
Foundation for an Individual Artist Grant awarded in 2015 in
addition to a Career Development Grant awarded in 2019. The
latter helped offset design and promotional costs of this book.

With gratitude also to mentors spanning many years includ-
ing: Jerry Wellik and the late Frank Kazemek, Diane Frank,
LouAnn Shepard Muhm, Mary Willette Hughes, Aimee Whit-
temore, and Alison McGhee.

I'm indebted to friends with whom I've traded countless po-
ems, most consistently: Susan Carlson, Ellen Lager, and Alan
Perry. From each of you, I've learned much, extending beyond
any perceived poemergency. Thank you to the League of MN
Poets, especially our local Grandview crew, and to Tracy Ritt-
mueller of Lyricality.org.

I've been richly blessed with the abiding friendship of Cheryl
Soltis, Tammy Nara, and Marcy Parent. I'm beholden to your
unwavering connection.

Thank you to Dan for keeping good humor under the bur-
den of relentless line break talk on top of the daily everything.
Thank you to Lily for all the ways you help me to see anew. I
am grateful to all of my family, then and now.

www.ingramcontent.com/pod-product-compliance
Lightning Source LLC
Chambersburg PA
CBHW031900090426
42741CB00005B/585